STARTING SPORT

Netball

Rebecca Hunter

Photography by Chris Fairclough

W

FRANKLIN WATTS

LONDON•SYDNEY

First published in 2006 by
Franklin Watts
338 Euston Road
London NW1 3BH

Franklin Watts Australia
Hachette Children's Books
Level 17/207 Kent Street
Sydney NSW 2000

© 2006 Franklin Watts

ISBN-10: 0 7496 6903 9
ISBN-13: 978 0 7496 6903 4

Dewey classification number: 796.324

A CIP catalogue record for this book is available
from the British Library.

Planning and production by Discovery Books Limited
Editor: Rebecca Hunter
Designer: Ian Winton
Photography: Chris Fairclough
Consultant: Leanne Willis, England Netball Level 2 qualified coach.

The author, packager and publisher would like to thank the following
people for their participation in this book: Leanne Willis and the pupils of
Packwood Haugh School, Shrewsbury, the Marches School, Oswestry and
Prestfelde School, Shrewsbury.

Printed in China

Franklin Watts is a division of Hachette Children's Books

Contents

The game of netball

Netball is a fast and exciting team sport that is played in many countries around the world.

Netball is usually played on a court by two teams of seven players. Younger players can play other versions of the game with fewer players (see pages 26–27).

Equipment

Netball is played with a ball the same size and weight as a football (size 5). It has a rougher surface than a football so it is easier to grip.

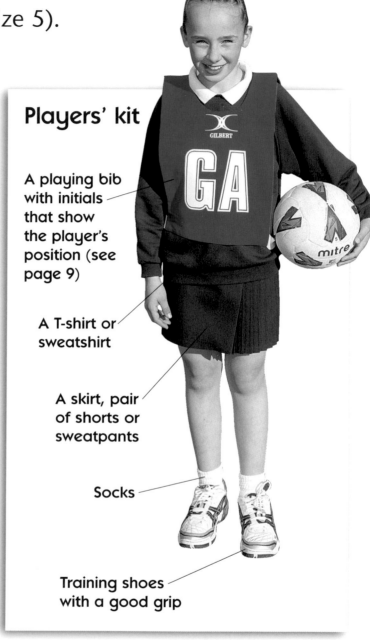

Players' kit

A playing bib with initials that show the player's position (see page 9)

A T-shirt or sweatshirt

A skirt, pair of shorts or sweatpants

Socks

Training shoes with a good grip

The aim of the game is to score more goals than the other team. Goals are scored by throwing the ball into rings fixed to posts at each end of the court.

The court and positions

A netball court can be indoors or outside. It is divided into three equal parts: two goal thirds and a centre third. In each goal third is the **goal circle**. This is actually a semi-circle around the goal post from where goals are scored.

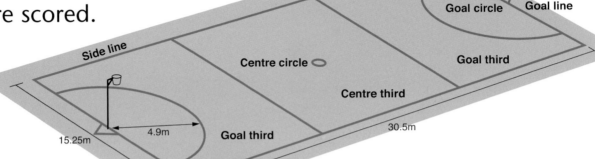

Goal post

Goal circle

Goal line

Centre circle

Goal third

Side line

Centre third

15.25m

4.9m

Goal third

30.5m

The goal post has a ring with a net attached to it. In the centre third is a **centre circle** where the game starts and restarts after a goal.

There are seven positions in a netball team. Each player wears a bib that shows their position.

8

The positions

Each player on a netball team has a special playing position and can only play in a certain area of the court.

Goal attack (GA): the GA is allowed to shoot goals and may play in the centre third as well as the goal third and the goal circle.

Goal defence (GD): the GD must help defend the goal circle from the opposition. She is allowed in her own goal third and goal circle, and the centre third.

Wing defence (WD): the WD's job is to defend against the opposition's WA. She may go in the centre third and her own goal third, but not her own goal circle.

Centre (C): the Centre can go anywhere on the court except the goal circles. The Centre has to be able to move quickly from defence to attack.

Goal shooter (GS): the GS is responsible for scoring goals. She is only allowed in the opposition's goal third, including the goal circle.

Goalkeeper (GK): The GK's job is to defend the goal. She should be tall and be able to jump high. She is only allowed in the goal third.

Wing attack (WA): the WA must be quick and ready to pass the ball to the shooters. She is allowed in the centre third and the opposition's goal third but not in the goal circle.

Playing a game

At the beginning of a game, only the two Centres are allowed to be in the centre third. All the other players must be in their own goal thirds.

The centre pass

The game starts with a centre pass from a Centre who must be standing inside the centre circle. The two team captains toss a coin to see which team takes the first centre pass. When the **umpire** blows the whistle, the Centre has three seconds to pass to a team mate.

Teamwork

Netball is a throwing and catching game and it takes good teamwork to move the ball about the court.

After catching a ball a player must either throw or bounce it once to another player within three seconds. There must be at least two passes after the centre pass before a goal can be scored.

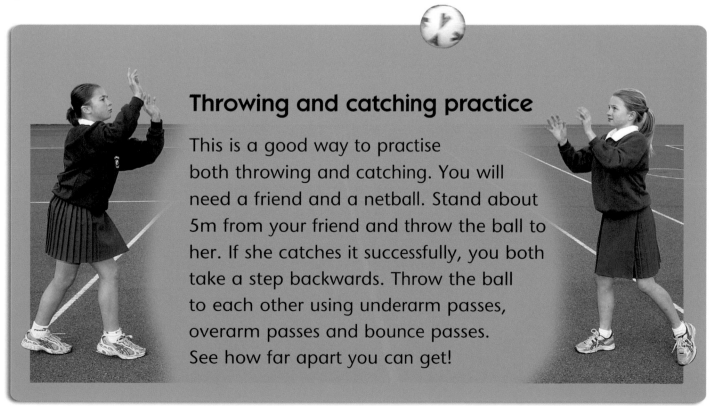

Throwing and catching practice

This is a good way to practise both throwing and catching. You will need a friend and a netball. Stand about 5m from your friend and throw the ball to her. If she catches it successfully, you both take a step backwards. Throw the ball to each other using underarm passes, overarm passes and bounce passes. See how far apart you can get!

Throwing

Being able to throw or pass well is one of the most important skills in netball.

Chest pass

For short distances, the easiest pass is a chest pass. This uses two hands. With your fingers spread around the ball and the thumbs behind it, throw the ball from your chest towards the chest of the player you are aiming at.

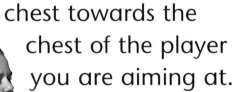

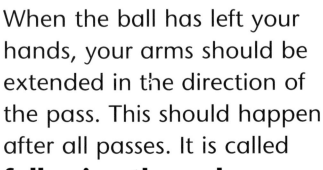

When the ball has left your hands, your arms should be extended in the direction of the pass. This should happen after all passes. It is called **following through**.

Shoulder pass

For longer distances, the shoulder pass is a better throw. This is a one-handed pass and is thrown from shoulder or head height. You take the ball in one hand and lean backwards as you raise it behind your shoulder. Spread your fingers out behind the ball and throw it forwards towards your team mate.

Overhead pass

This pass is useful for throwing the ball over very tall **opponents**. Hold both sides of the ball above and just behind your head. Stretch up and release the ball at the highest point so it goes as high as possible.

Catching

To be a good catcher you need to be in the right place at the right time and to keep your eyes on the ball all the time.

Basic two-handed catch

As the ball comes towards you, watch it carefully and stretch out your arms to receive it.

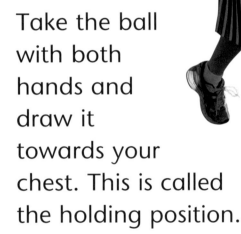

Take the ball with both hands and draw it towards your chest. This is called the holding position.

One-handed catching

Sometimes it is not possible to catch the ball with two hands so one-handed catching is a good skill to learn. It is important to practise one-handed catching with both of your hands. You will need to jump high and stretch out your arms.

Footwork rule

Netball players are not allowed to run with the ball but they can move their feet according to the footwork rule.

Landing foot

When a player catches the ball in the air (**1**), the first foot to touch the ground is called the landing foot (**2**). The player may then step with the other foot in any direction (**3**). She may then lift the landing foot but must throw or shoot the ball before this foot touches the ground again.

Shooting

The **attacking** players pass the ball down the court into the opponent's goal circle. Then the next move is for a goal to be attempted. Only two players, the Goal Shooter and Goal Attack are allowed to shoot goals.

The static shot

When preparing to shoot, hold the ball as high as possible. This will make it harder for the defenders to reach it.

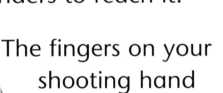

The fingers on your shooting hand should be pointing backwards spread under the ball. Your other hand should be at the side of the ball to control it.

Bend your knees, then straighten up whilst extending your arms. Release the ball as high as possible so that it drops easily into the ring.

Step and shoot

Sometimes you may have to step forwards, backwards or sideways in order to get into a position to shoot. Remember to move your feet so as to stay within the footwork rule (see page 15).

The Goalkeeper and Goal Defence will try to stop their opponents shooting a goal. They may jump to intercept a shot but must not be closer to the shooter than 0.9m.

Pig in the middle

This is good for practising both shooting and defence skills. You will need between eight and twelve people. Make a circle of about six to ten people, with two or three players in the middle. Throw the ball across the circle from player to player whilst the inside players try to intercept. If a centre player catches the ball, she changes places with the thrower.

Rules and penalties

As with all games, netball players must obey the rules and any rule breaking is penalized. The umpire will blow the whistle to stop the game and award one of the following.

Penalty pass

A penalty pass is given when a player contacts or obstructs another player. Contact is when players bump or run into each other. Obstruction is when a player gets too close to the player with the ball.

The penalty pass is taken from the spot where the rule was broken. The player who committed the offence must stand next to their partner while they make the pass (see right).

Toss-up

If two players break a rule at the same time, the umpire awards a toss-up. The two players face each other 0.9m apart. The umpire blows the whistle and throws the ball up between the players. They have to jump to catch or push the ball.

Free pass

A free pass is given for footwork faults and when a player goes offside (when a player goes outside their correct playing area). In this picture, the Centre has wrongly stepped into the goal circle.

Throw-in

If you throw the ball out of the court a throw-in is awarded to the opposition's team. The throw-in is taken from outside the court close to the line. The player must throw the ball before stepping back on to the court.

Attack

Out of the seven players in a netball team, three are attacking players, three are defence players and the centre can play as either.

Netball is all about getting the ball down to the goal circle so that your goalscorers can shoot a goal. The attacking players, Goal Attack and Wing Attack, must be fast around the court. They need to get into a position where they can receive the ball and pass it on to another player. This is called **getting free**.

Holding a space

Sometimes a player may 'hold a space' on the court. This means they stand still and use their body to prevent the defenders moving into that space. Shooters often use this skill, standing in a good position by the goal, until they can turn and receive the ball from a team mate. They then have a good chance to shoot a goal from their chosen spot.

Dodge ball

This helps players to learn how to dodge quickly and practise the quick, unexpected movements that attacking players use. You will need at least ten friends to play this game. The players stand in a circle with two or three in the middle. Using two netballs, the players on the outside try to throw the ball to hit the centre players below the knee. The middle players must dodge and move to avoid this. When a player is hit, the thrower swaps places with her.

Defence

In a game of netball having good defence players is just as important as having good attacking players.

Marking

Defenders must stick close to their opponents or **mark** them. If you are a defence player you should:

- shadow your opponent's movements at all times
- make it hard for them to break free and receive a pass
- watch the ball closely and, if it is thrown to your opponent, try to intercept the pass
- not be closer than 0.9m to your opponent
- either reach out in front of the player to get the ball, or jump to intercept it.

Defending goals

Goalkeepers and Goal Defences must be good at intercepting goal shots. They need good balance to be able to stretch up in front of the shooter, and they need to be able to jump well to deflect a ball that is heading for the goal.

One-on-one marking

With one-on-one marking, each player in the team takes responsibility for covering one opponent. Using their defensive skills, the defender must block and mark their opponents and force them into less useful areas of the court.

Warming up

Netball is an active sport. To play well for the length of a game without getting tired, you need to be fit and healthy.

Before playing a game of netball, you should spend about 5-10 minutes warming up with exercises like these.

1. Stand on one leg and raise your other leg up behind you. Hold this leg and pull gently. Feel the stretch in the upper thigh of your bent leg. Do the same with the other leg.

2. Lunge forward on your right leg. Your left leg should be bent with your knee nearly touching the ground. Press down with your hands on your thigh. Repeat with the other leg.

3. Raise your right leg with knee bent. Press down on your right thigh. Hold this position for a count of 10. Repeat with the other leg.

Jog and sprint drill

Stand at the end of the court, on the line near the goal. Sprint to the line that marks out the first third of the court. Jog back. Now sprint to the next line of the centre third. Jog back again. Finally sprint to the end of the court and jog back.

Ball handling

Before starting the game practise some ball handling skills with your team mates.

Junior games

To make netball easier to learn, there are some different versions of the game for younger players to play.

First Steps Netball

First Steps Netball is a game for seven to nine year olds. There are four players on each team. The playing area is smaller – only one third of a full-size court. The goal posts are shorter and a smaller ball (size 4) is used. A First Steps game is much shorter than a normal game.

High Five Netball

Many children in the nine to eleven year old age group play High Five Netball. This game provides a good link between First Steps Netball and the full 7 a-side rules.

High Five Netball has a normal sized court, a slightly shorter goal post and also uses a size 4 ball. The game is played with four quarters of 6 minutes each. A High Five squad has between seven and nine players, although only five are on the court at any one time.

Players take it in turns to be playing on the court or to be scorers, timekeepers or **centre pass markers**.

During the 2-minute intervals between each quarter, the players' positions are rotated so they play in several positions. All players get the experience of playing both defensive and attacking positions.

Glossary

attacking any moves made by players while they have the ball and are moving towards their goal end to score.

centre circle the circle in the centre of the court. It is 0.9m in diameter.

centre pass marker a player who keeps track of which centre player should take the next centre pass.

following through the position of the arms, hands and fingers as the player releases the ball.

getting free getting into a position where you can receive the ball.

goal circle the area inside the semi-circle that is 4.9m away from the goal post.

mark stay close to your opposite player and shadow her movements.

opponent a player on the other team.

umpire the person who controls the game and makes sure players play by the rules.

Further reading

Netball: Know the Game, A & C Black, October 2006

Youth Netball: Age 7-11 101 Youth Drills, Chris Sheryn, Anna Sheryn, A & C Black, 2005

Essential Sports: Netball, Andy Smith, Heinemann Library, 2004

Netball: Steps to Success, Wilma Shakespear, Human Kinetics Europe Ltd, 1997

Netball: Skills of the Game, Betty Galsworthy, The Crowood Press Ltd, 1996

Further information

England Netball
Netball House
9 Paynes Park
Hitchin,
Hertfordshire
England
SG5 1EH
Email: info@englandnetball.co.uk
Website: www.england-netball.co.uk

International Netball Federation
Belle Vue Leisure Centre
Kirkmanshulme Lane
Longsight
Manchester
England
M12 4TF
Email: ifna@netball.org
Website: www.netball.org

Netball Australia
43-45 Marion Street
Harris Park NSW 2150
Australia
Email: infonet@netball.asn.au
Website: www.netball.asn.au

Australian Sports Commission
PO Box 176
Belconnen ACT 2616
Australia
Email: club.development@ausport.gov.au
Website: www.ausport.gov.au

Index